Student Interactive

myView

LITERACY

SAVVAS
LEARNING COMPANY

ISBN-13: 978-0-134-90870-0
ISBN-10: 0-134-90870-8

12 23

Julie Coiro, Ph.D.

Jim Cummins, Ph.D.

Pat Cunningham, Ph.D.

Elfrieda Hiebert, Ph.D.

Pamela Mason, Ed.D.

Ernest Morrell, Ph.D.

P. David Pearson, Ph.D.

Frank Serafini, Ph.D.

Alfred Tatum, Ph.D.

Sharon Vaughn, Ph.D.

Judy Wallis, Ed.D.

Lee Wright, Ed.D.

Living Together

Genre | Informational Text

WEEK 1

READING WORKSHOP

Infographic: Time to Move!

FOUNDATIONAL SKILLS Consonant Dd • Consonant Kk 16

Animals on the Move ..... Informational Text 31
by Ron Fridell

Reading Comprehension • Find Main Idea and Supporting Details

READING-WRITING BRIDGE 45

Academic Vocabulary • Pre-Spelling: Rhyming Sort • Read Like a Writer, Write for a Reader • Language and Conventions: Adjectives and Articles

WRITING WORKSHOP 49

Plan Your List Book

WEEK 2

READING WORKSHOP

Infographic: Making a Place to Live

FOUNDATIONAL SKILLS Short o Spelled o • Consonant Ff 54

From Nectar to Honey ..... Informational Text 69
by Christine Taylor-Butler

Reading Comprehension • Find Text Structure

READING-WRITING BRIDGE 83

Academic Vocabulary • Pre-Spelling: Rhyming Sort • Read Like a Writer, Write for a Reader • Language and Conventions: Adjectives and Articles

WRITING WORKSHOP 87

Write Your List Book

WEEK 3

Genre | Fiction

READING WORKSHOP
Diagram: Eating Well

FOUNDATIONAL SKILLS Consonant Hh • Consonant Ll 92

Do We Need This?...Fiction 107
by Guadalupe V. Lopez

Reading Comprehension • Identify and Describe Characters

READING-WRITING BRIDGE 121

Academic Vocabulary • Pre-Spelling: Rhyming Sort • Read Like a Writer,
Write for a Reader • Language and Conventions: Verbs

WRITING WORKSHOP 125

Organize Your List Book

WEEK 4

Genre | Informational Text

READING WORKSHOP
Infographic: How Anteaters Eat

FOUNDATIONAL SKILLS Consonant Gg • Consonant Blends 130

Open Wide!...Informational Text 145
by Ana Galán

Reading Comprehension • Find Text Features

READING-WRITING BRIDGE 159

Academic Vocabulary • Pre-Spelling: Rhyming Sort • Read Like a Writer,
Write for a Reader • Language and Conventions: Verbs

WRITING WORKSHOP 163

Edit Your List Book

WEEK 5

Genre | Persuasive Text

READING WORKSHOP
Poem: Let's Exercise!

FOUNDATIONAL SKILLS Short e Spelled e • Consonants Ww and Yy 168

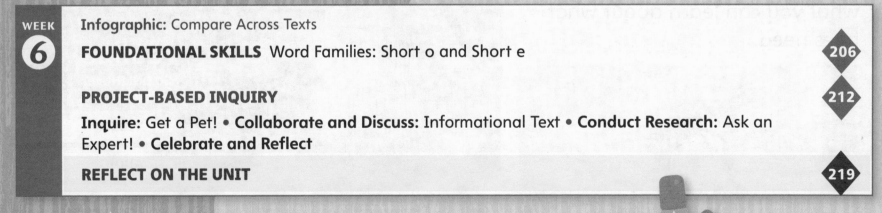

Run, Jump, and Swim .... Persuasive Text 183
by Kimberly Feltes Taylor

Reading Comprehension • Find Text Structure

READING-WRITING BRIDGE 197
Academic Vocabulary • Pre-Spelling: Rhyming Sort • Read Like a Writer,
Write for a Reader • Language and Conventions: Verbs

WRITING WORKSHOP 201
Share Your List Book

WEEK 6

Infographic: Compare Across Texts
FOUNDATIONAL SKILLS Word Families: Short o and Short e 206

PROJECT-BASED INQUIRY 212
Inquire: Get a Pet! • **Collaborate and Discuss:** Informational Text • **Conduct Research:** Ask an
Expert! • **Celebrate and Reflect**

REFLECT ON THE UNIT 219

UNIT 2

Living Together

Essential Question

What do living things need?

▶ **Watch**

"**Buzz, Buzz, Buzz!**" and see what you can learn about what bees need.

 **TURN and TALK**

What do bees need?

SAVVAS
realize™
Go ONLINE for
all lessons.

▶ VIDEO

◀)) AUDIO

GAME

ANNOTATE

BOOK

RESEARCH

Spotlight on Informational Text

Reading Workshop

Infographic: Time to Move!

Animals on the Move .... Informational Text
by Ron Fridell

Infographic: Making a Place to Live

From Nectar to Honey .... Informational Text
by Christine Taylor-Butler

Diagram: Eating Well

Do We Need This? .... Fiction
by Guadalupe V. Lopez

Infographic: How Anteaters Eat

Open Wide! .... Informational Text
by Ana Galán

Poem: Let's Exercise!

Run, Jump, and Swim .... Persuasive Text
by Kimberly Feltes Taylor

Reading-Writing Bridge

• Academic Vocabulary • Pre-Spelling • Read Like a Writer,
Write for a Reader • Language and Conventions

Writing Workshop

• Plan Your List Book • Compose Details • Organize Ideas   **Informational Text**
• Edit for Adjectives • Publish and Celebrate

Project-Based Inquiry

• Inquire • Research • Collaborate

Read Together

Independent Reading

Follow these steps to read on your own!

1. Choose a book.

2. Start at the front cover.

3. Turn the pages gently.

4. Put the book back when you are finished.

Directions Tell students they should choose a book that does not look too easy or too hard. Discuss how to handle a book properly. Say: Make sure you are holding the book right side up. When you finish a page, turn gently to the next page. Have students practice the skills as they self-select and interact independently with text.

My Independent Reading Log

Date	Book	Pages Read	My Ratings
			😊 😐 🙁
			😊 😐 🙁
			😊 😐 🙁
			😊 😐 🙁

Directions Have students complete the chart to tell about their independent reading.

Unit Goals

In this unit, you will

○ read informational texts

△ write an informational text

□ learn about living things

 **MY TURN** (Circle) living things.

Directions Read the unit goals to students. Then discuss the difference between living and non-living things. Have students circle the pictures that show living things.

Academic Vocabulary

| grow | need | share | depend |

Animals **need** food to **grow**.

Some animals **share** food with each other.

They **depend** on one another.

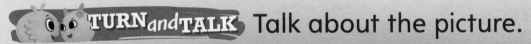 Talk about the picture.

Directions Read the Academic Vocabulary words and the sentences to students. Say: You can use words you learn to talk about ideas and texts. Have students use the newly acquired Academic Vocabulary to talk about the picture with a partner.

13

Read Together

Time to Move!

This is a whooping crane.

In the summer it lives in the north.

Then the weather gets cold.
The whooping crane needs
to go somewhere warm.

Where does it go?

14

Weekly Question

Why do some animals move from place to place?

Canada

United States

N
W · E
S

🦉🦉 **TURN** *and* **TALK** Talk about the map.

Directions Read the text and have students look at the map. Explain how to use the compass to identify north and south. Ask students to talk about what the map shows. Then have them answer the Weekly Question.

15

Initial and Final Sounds

 Circle

 Underline

16

Directions Say: Listen to the sound at the beginning of this word: /d/ -og. *Dog* has the sound /d/ at the beginning. Have students circle the picture words in the first row that begin with the sound /d/ like *dog*. Continue with the second row, asking students to underline the picture words that end with the sound /d/ like *wood*.

Consonant Dd

 Circle

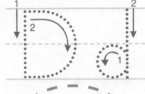   

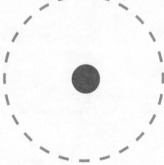   

Directions Tell students that the letter *d* makes the sound /d/. Say: You will see the letter *d* in words that have the /d/ sound. Model how to form the letters *D* and *d*. Have students trace the letters *Dd* and identify the sound *d* represents. Say: Now you will match the letter and the sound. Circle the picture words that begin or end with the sound for *d*.

17

Consonant Dd

 Read and write

dip

sad

pad

18

Directions Have students trace the letter *d* in each word and say the sound for the letter. Then have them use what they know about letters and sounds to read each word. Finally, have students write the words on the lines.

Final Sounds

 Circle

Directions Have students name each picture and circle the picture words that end with the sound /k/. Model: Listen to the sounds in this word: /r/ /o/ /k/. The sound at the end of *rock* is /k/.

Consonant Kk

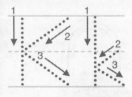

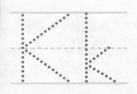

Directions Tell students that the letter *k* makes the sound /k/. Explain that they will see the letter *k* in many words that have the /k/ sound. Model how to form the letters *K* and *k*. Have students trace the letters *Kk* and identify the sound that *k* represents. Say: Now you will match the letter and the sound. Circle the picture words in each row that begin with the sound for *k*.

20

My Words to Know

| of | are | that |

My Sentences to Read

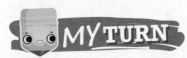

We a<u>r</u>e with Kim.

Can we have a bit of that?

Directions Say: There are some words that we have to remember and practice. Listen to these words: *of, are, that*. Have students point to each word as they read it aloud. Then have students read the sentences. Ask them to identify and underline the high-frequency words in the sentences.

Consonant Kk

 Read and match

kid

kit

Kim

Directions Have students trace the letter *K* or *k* in each word and say the sound for the letter. Then ask them to read each word and draw a line from the word to the matching picture.

The Kid

Highlight the words with the d sound.

We are sad!

AUDIO

Audio with Highlighting

ANNOTATE

23

Dan, I see that <u>kid</u>.

Kip, I see that can.

Underline the words with the letter **k.**

We ran to the kid.

Can we have a sip of that?

25

Consonants Dd and Kk

 **TURN** *and* **TALK** Read

 **pad** **dab**

 **kid** **Kip**

 **kit** **Kim**

 **Dan** **dad**

26

Directions Remind students that the letter *d* makes the sound /d/ and the letter *k* makes the sound /k/. Have partners take turns pointing to the letter *d* or *k* in each word and saying the sound for the letter. Then have partners take turns reading the words.

Consonants Dd and Kk

  Read and write

dip	kid

Look at Kim.

_____

She is a _____.

_____

She can _____ it.

Directions Remind students that the letter *d* makes the sound /d/ and the letter *k* makes the sound /k/. Have students read the words in the word bank. Then have them read the sentences. Ask students to complete each sentence by writing the best word from the word bank on the lines.

27

My Learning Goal

I can read informational text.

SPOTLIGHT ON GENRE

Informational Text

An **informational text** tells details about a central, or main, idea.

Main Idea → Birds have body parts that help them.

Details → Their wings help them fly.

Their beak helps them eat.

TURN and TALK Talk about other details that would be in an informational text about birds.

28

Directions Read aloud the model text. Say: The main idea is what the text is mostly about. Supporting evidence, or details, tell more about the main idea. Have students identify the main idea and supporting evidence in the model text and think of other details an informational text about birds might tell.

Informational Text Anchor Chart

Detail

Detail

Main Idea

Detail

Animals on the Move

Preview Vocabulary

butterflies

geese

whales

Read

Read the text to learn why animals move from one place to another.

Meet the Author

Ron Fridell writes books about pumpkins, silkworms, rivers, and jungles. He loves to hike, climb, and visit faraway places. He tries to make each day an exciting adventure.

30

Animals on the Move

written by Ron Fridell

AUDIO

Audio with Highlighting

ANNOTATE

Some animals need
to take long trips.
They travel, or migrate,
for different reasons.

CLOSE READ

What do some animals do? Underline the word that names the main idea.

Butterflies, geese, and whales migrate.

Why do animals migrate?
They need to get away
from places that are cold.

CLOSE READ

Why do animals migrate? Highlight the words that answer the question.

Why do monarch butterflies migrate? Monarch butterflies fly south just to stay alive.

35

Why do geese migrate?
Geese fly to warm places
to find food.

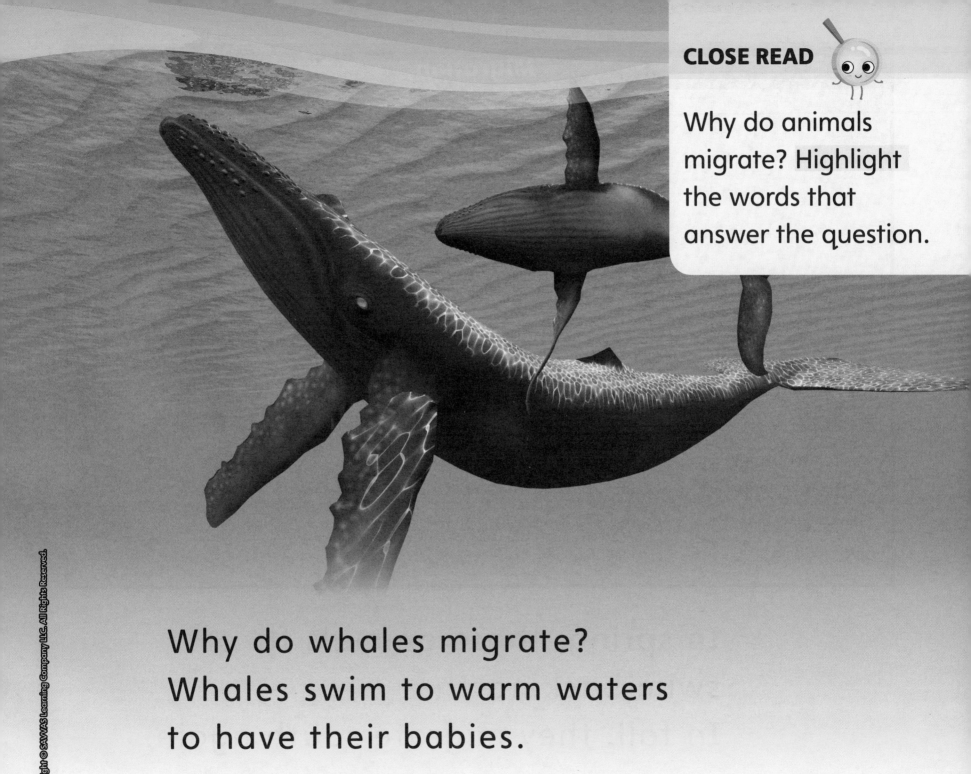

CLOSE READ

Why do animals migrate? Highlight the words that answer the question.

Why do whales migrate?
Whales swim to warm waters
to have their babies.

37

Migration

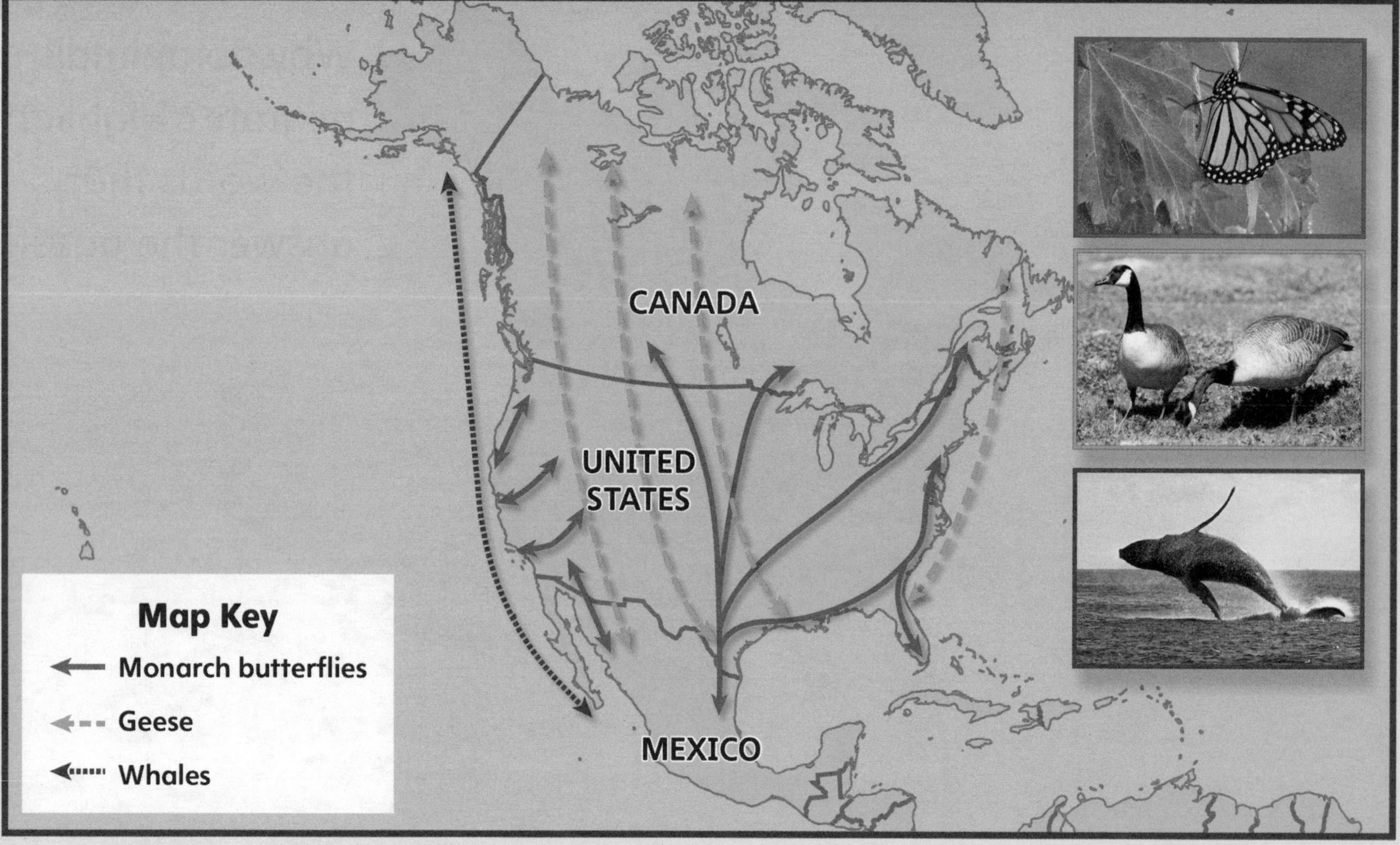

CANADA

UNITED STATES

MEXICO

Map Key

← Monarch butterflies

←-- Geese

←···· Whales

In spring, these animals fly or swim back north.
In fall, they migrate south again.

CLOSE READ

What do animals do in the spring? Highlight the words that answer the question.

Would you want to get away from cold weather?
Where would you go?

39

Develop Vocabulary

 Draw

butterflies	geese	whales

40

Directions Read the vocabulary words to students. Then have them draw a picture to show the meaning of each word.

Read
Together

Check for Understanding

 Write

1. One fact I learned is

_____

- -

_____.

2. Why does the author include pictures?

_____

- -

_____

3. Why do animals need to go to warm places?

_____

- -

_____

Directions Read aloud the items one at a time and have students write their responses. Remind them to use text evidence.

Find Main Idea and Supporting Evidence

The **main idea** is what the text is mostly about. **Supporting evidence,** or details, tells more about the main idea.

 Write and (circle)

_____

- -

_____

42

Directions Read aloud the sentences at the top of the page. Have students look back at the text to find the main idea and details that tell about the main idea. Say: Write a word that names the main idea. Circle the picture that shows evidence that supports the main idea.

Make Inferences

You can use details in the text and what you already know to **make inferences**.

 Draw

Directions Read aloud the information at the top of the page. Say: Why do the animals go north again in the spring? Draw a picture to show the answer. Have students look back at the text. Remind them to use what they already know and evidence from the text to support their understanding.

Reflect and Share

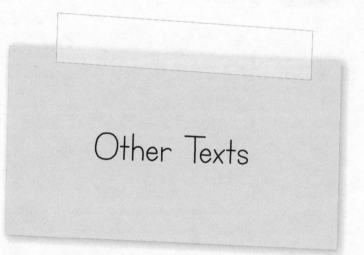 **TURN and TALK** Tell the main idea and important details from the text. How is it similar to other texts you have read about animals?

Animals on the Move

Other Texts

Weekly Question

Why do some animals move from place to place?

44

Directions Have partners take turns retelling the text. Say: When you retell a text, you tell the most important details. Then have partners respond to sources by comparing the text with other texts they have read about animals.

I can use words to tell about informational text.

Academic Vocabulary

grow	need	share	depend

 Circle

The bird shared some food last night.

Now it needs to find more.

Directions Remind students that the endings *-s* and *-ed* can be added to the ends of some verbs. Read aloud the sentences one at a time. Ask students to circle the word in each sentence that has an ending added to it.

Rhyming Sort

 Match

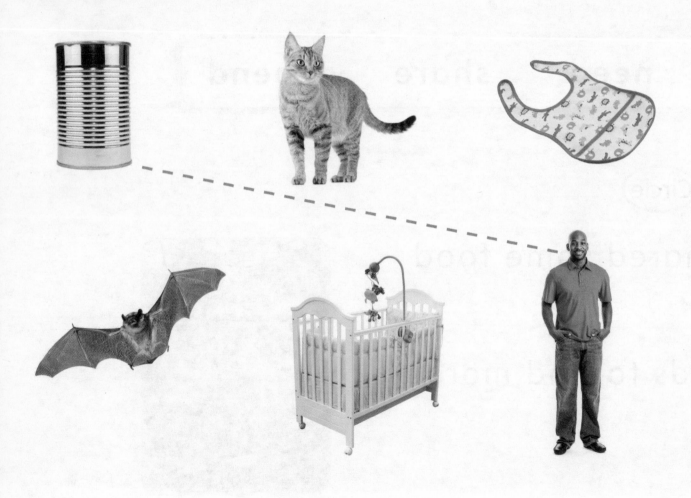

46

Directions Have students name the pictures. Say: Rhyming words are words that have the same middle and ending sounds. Ask students to identify the rhyming words by drawing a line from each word in the first row to the picture word that rhymes in the second row. Then ask them to produce rhyming words by saying other words that rhyme with one of the pairs. Model: The word *rat* rhymes with *cat* and *bat*.

Read Like a Writer, Write for a Reader

 Write

_____

1. The author asks _____ and

   _____

   gives _____.

 Ask questions.

2.

Directions Read the first item and have students write their responses on the lines. Say: Authors organize texts in different ways. They choose a structure, or way of organizing, that helps them. Discuss with students how the question and answer structure contributes to the author's purpose. Then have students look at the picture and take turns asking questions about the picture with a partner.

Read Together

Adjectives and Articles

An **adjective** describes something.

The words **a**, **an**, and **the** are articles.

This is **a big** whale.

 Tell what the whale looks like.

 Write

| a | the | gray | small |

_____ _____

Look at _____ _____ skin.

48

Directions Read the information and have partners discuss what the whale looks like. Then read the articles, adjectives, and sentence. Have students edit the sentence by writing the best article and descriptive adjective on the lines.

I can write an informational text.

My Learning Goal

List Book

A **list book** has a title.

A list book gives details about a main idea.

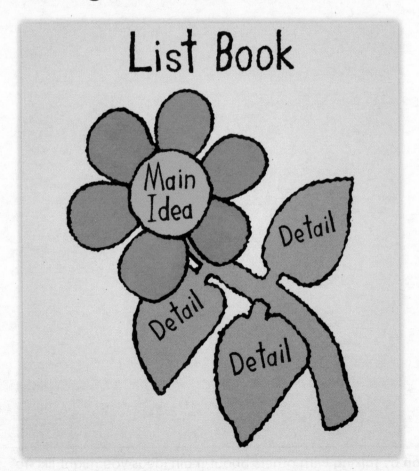

Directions Read the text on the anchor chart to students. Discuss the characteristics of a list book.

49

Generate Ideas

A **main idea** is what a book is all about.

 Draw

50

Directions Say: Before you write, you can plan by talking with others about main ideas you might like to write about. Have students generate ideas for writing through class discussion. After the discussion, have students draw to show main ideas they like.

Plan Your List Book

Authors plan what they will write about a main idea.

 Draw

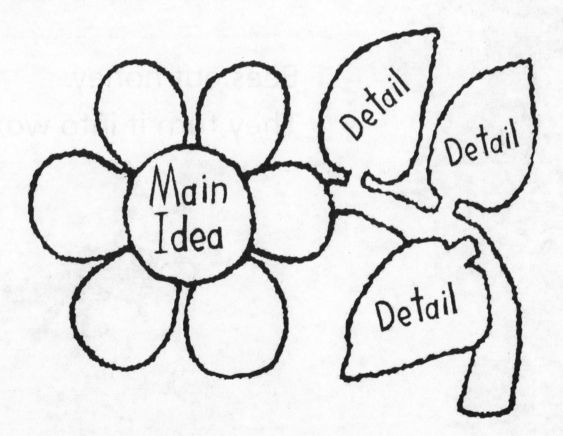

Directions Ask the class to generate main ideas for a list book as you draw the ideas on the board. Then have students choose a main idea and draw it in the flower. Say: Now you can plan what you will write about the main idea. What are some details, or examples, you can put in your list book? Have students generate ideas for writing by drawing details on the leaves.

51

Making a Place to Live

Bees live in a hive.

1 Bees eat honey.
They turn it into wax.

How do some living things make what they need?

3 Bees use the wax to build the hive and honeycombs.

2 Bees chew the wax to make it soft.

TURN and TALK Talk about the text and the pictures.

53

Directions Read the text to students as they look at the pictures. Have students use the text and pictures to tell about how bees make their home.

Sounds

 Circle

54

Directions Model: Listen to the sounds in this word: /s/ /o/ /k/, *sock*. *Sock* has the sound /o/ in the middle. Have students segment and blend the sounds in each picture word, circling the ones with the sound /o/ in the middle.

Short o Spelled o

 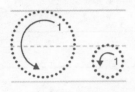

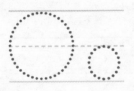

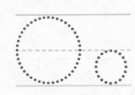

Directions Tell students that the letter *o* can make the sound /o/. Model how to form the letters *O* and *o*. Say: You will see the letter *o* in many words that have the short *o* sound. Trace the letters *Oo*. Point to the letter *o* and identify, or tell me, the sound it makes. Now circle each picture word that has the same *o* sound in the middle.

55

Short o Spelled o

 Read and write

m o p

d o t

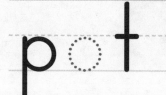

p o t

56

Directions Have students name the pictures and trace the letter *o* in each word. Then have them decode and write each word.

Alliteration

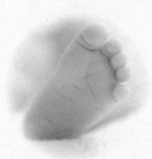

Directions Say: Some groups of words begin with the same sound. Listen to this word: /f/-ork, *fork*. Which picture words begin with the same sound as *fork*? Have students recognize alliteration by circling the picture words with the same initial sound.

57

Consonant Ff

 MY TURN (Circle)

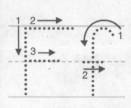   

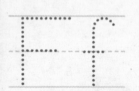   

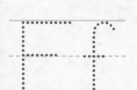   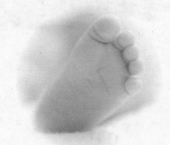

Directions Tell students that the letter *f* makes the sound /f/. Model how to form the letters *F* and *f*. Say: You will see the letter *f* in many words that have the /f/ sound. Trace the letters *Ff*. Point to the letter *f* and identify, or tell me, the sound it makes. Now circle each picture word that begins with the same /f/ sound.

My Words to Know

| do | you | they |

My Sentences to Read

They have a dog.

Do you like the house?

Directions Say: There are some words that we have to remember and practice, such as *do*. **Have students read the high-frequency words. Then have them read the sentences and underline the high-frequency words in the sentences.**

Consonant Ff

 Read and write

 f an

 f it

 f in

60

Directions Have students name the pictures and trace the letter *f* in each word. Then have them decode and write each word.

Bob on the Mat

Highlight the words with the short **o** sound.

Look at Bob.

He is with Tif.

AUDIO
Audio with Highlighting

ANNOTATE

61

Look, <u>Tif</u>! Bob is at the mat.

They like the mat. Do you like it?

Underline the words
with the **f** sound.

Bob sat.

Bob can fit on the mat.

63

Short o and Consonant Ff

 Read

 fig   **fan**   **fib**

 fad   **fin**   **fat**

 cot   **top**   **nod**

 not   **mop**   **dot**

Directions Remind students that the letter *o* can make the sound /o/ and the letter *f* makes the sound /f/. Then have students take turns reading the words with a partner.

Short o and Consonant Ff

 **MY TURN** (Circle) and underline

(Tom) is fit.

Do you see the mop?

The fan is not on.

Do you have a pot?

Directions Remind students that the letter o can make the sound /o/ and the letter f makes the sound /f/. Have students circle the words with short o and underline the words with the letter f. Then have them read the sentences.

65

My Learning Goal

I can read informational text.

SPOTLIGHT ON GENRE

Informational Text

An informational text can tell how something happens.

It can tell **steps in a sequence**, or what happens first, next, and last.

First   **Next**   **Last**

 Retell the steps in order.

Directions Read the genre information to students. Say: Remember that informational texts tell details about a central, or main, idea. Sometimes those details tell the steps in a sequence. Have students discuss how a flower grows. Then have partners take turns retelling the steps in order.

Informational Text Anchor Chart

Step 1

Step 2

Step 3

From Nectar to Honey

Preview Vocabulary

bees	honey	nectar	hive

Read

Listen to the title and look at the picture. What questions do you have before you read the text?

Meet the Author

Christine Taylor-Butler has written more than 75 books for children. She has won prizes for her books. In school Christine studied engineering, art, and design. She now lives in Kansas City.

Directions Remind students that they can ask questions about a text before they read it. Say: Asking and answering questions before, during, and after reading can help you better understand a text and get information. Have students look at the photo on the title page and ask questions about the text before reading.

Read Together

Genre Informational Text

 AUDIO

Audio with Highlighting

 ANNOTATE

From Nectar to Honey

written by
Christine Taylor-Butler

Did you know that flowers
help bees?
They help bees make honey.

Copyright © SAVVAS Learning Company LLC. All Rights Reserved.

bee

flower

Bees fly many miles each day. They fly from one flower to another.

nectar

First, flowers make a sweet juice called nectar.
Next, bees sip the nectar.

CLOSE READ

How do flowers help bees make honey? Underline the words that tell when the steps happen.

wings

head

antennae

stomach

legs

Bees store the nectar in their stomachs.

hive

Bees sip the nectar until
they are full.
After that, they fly back
to the hive.

74

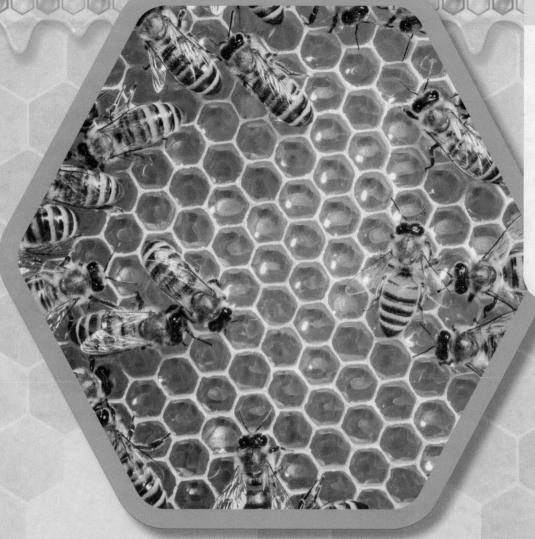

CLOSE READ

What questions can you ask about the steps on these pages? Highlight the answers to your questions.

Other bees work in the hive. Then they turn the nectar into honey.

75

honey

Bees store the honey
in their hives.
They eat the honey in winter.

76

We can eat the honey too!

Develop Vocabulary

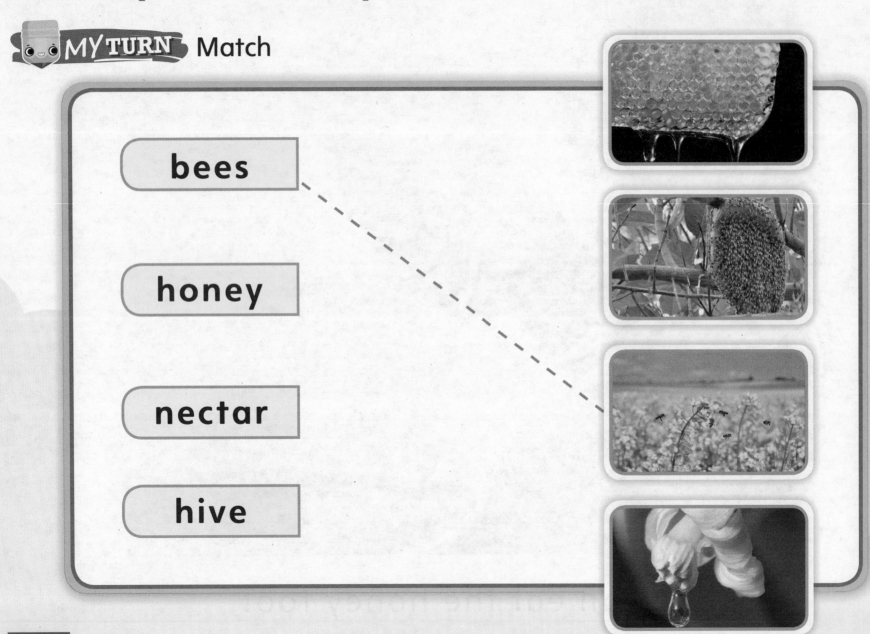

MY TURN Match

bees

honey

nectar

hive

Directions Read the words to students. Have them use illustrations to clarify word meanings by drawing a line from each word to the matching picture.

Check for Understanding

  **MY TURN** (Circle) and write

1. What is the main idea?

2. Why does the author use the words *first* and *next?*

_____

_____

_____

3. Why do bees need to fly many miles each day?

_____

_____

_____

Directions Read aloud question 1 and the answer choices to students. Have them circle the answer. Then read aloud questions 2 and 3 and encourage students to write their answers.

79

Find Text Structure

 Draw and write

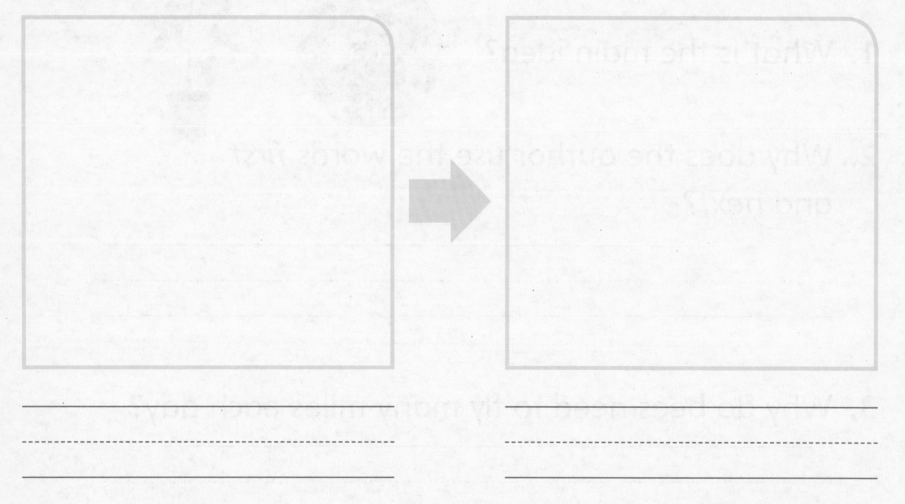

80

Directions Say: Some informational texts tell the steps in a sequence, or what happens first, next, and last. Have students draw pictures to show how flowers help bees make honey. Then have them label the steps with sequence words. Remind students to look back at the text.

Ask and Answer Questions

 **Draw**

Directions Remind students that they can ask and answer questions before, during, and after they read to help them better understand the text and get information. Have students generate a question about the text and share it with a partner. Then have them draw to show the answer to their question. Remind students to look back at the text.

Reflect and Share

 Draw

Weekly Question

How do some living things make what they need?

Directions Tell students they read about bees. Ask: What other animals have you read about? Have students respond to sources by drawing a bee and another animal they have read about.

Read Together

I can use words to tell about informational text.

Academic Vocabulary

| grow | need | share | depend |

 Match

share   shrink

grow   keep

Directions Read the words to students. Have them match each word on the left to the word on the right that has the opposite meaning.

Rhyming Sort

 MY TURN Match

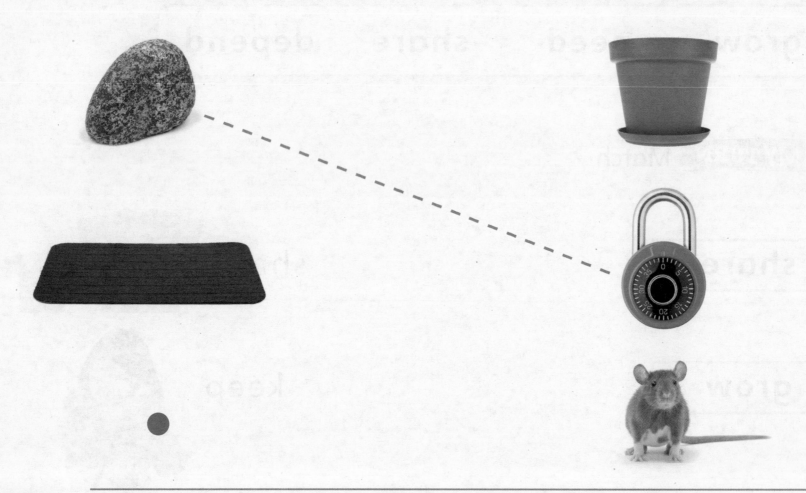

84

Directions Tell students that rhyming words have the same middle and ending sounds. Have them identify rhyming words by drawing a line to match each picture word on the left with the rhyming picture word on the right. Then ask students to produce rhyming words by saying other words that rhyme with one of the word pairs. **Model:** The word *sock* rhymes with *rock* and *lock*.

Read Like a Writer, Write for a Reader

 Write

1. Find a word in the text that helps you picture nectar.

_____

- -

_____

2. What word could you add to the text to help readers picture a bee?

_____

- -

_____

Directions Discuss with students how authors use words that help readers visualize, or picture, something in their minds. Read the first item with students. Have them look back at the text to find the answer and then write it on the line. Then read the second item and have students write their response. Encourage them to look at the photos in the text for ideas.

Read Together

Adjectives and Articles

An **adjective** describes something.

The words **a**, **an**, and **the** are articles.

Look at **the yellow** flower.

 Write

a	the	pointy	long

The flower has stem.

_____

- - - - - - - - - - - - - - - - - -

_____

Directions Read the information at the top of the page. Then read aloud the words and the sentence. Have students edit the sentence by rewriting it on the lines, adding an article and a descriptive adjective to tell about the stem.

I can write an informational text.

My Learning Goal

Compose a Title

A **title** tells what the text is about.

 **MY TURN** Write

_____

- -

_____

A bird builds a nest.

It uses sticks.

It uses leaves.

It even uses feathers.

Directions Read the text to students. Have them dictate or compose a title for the informational text.

Main Idea

The **central,** or **main, idea** is the most important thing the author writes about.

 MY TURN Circle

88

Directions Read the model text about a bird building a nest to students. Have them think about the main idea of the text. Then ask students to circle the picture that shows the main idea.

Compose Details

Details tell more about the central, or main, idea.

 **MY TURN** Draw or write

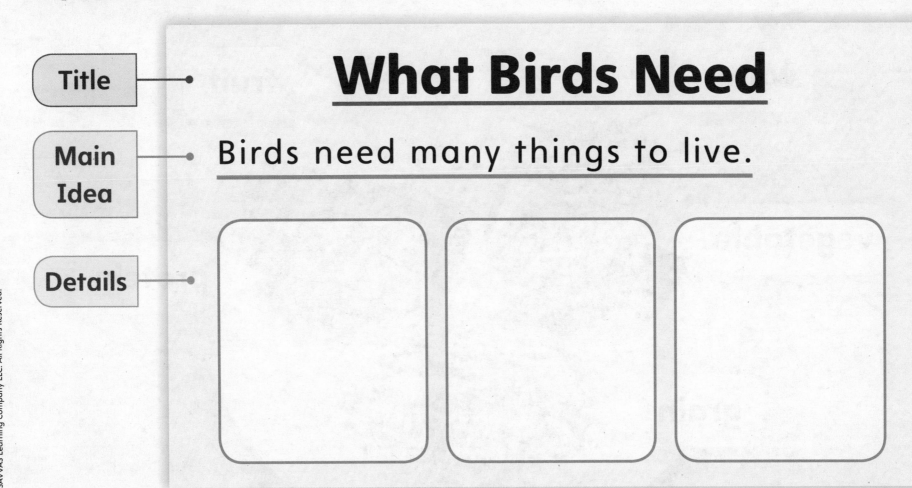

Title •—— <u>**What Birds Need**</u>

Main Idea •—— <u>Birds need many things to live.</u>

Details •——

Directions Have students dictate, compose, or draw details that support the main idea.

Read Together

Eating Well

We need to eat good food to stay healthy.

water

fruit

vegetable

protein

grain

90

Weekly Question

How do we know what we need?

 **MY TURN** Write

vegetable	fruit	grain

Directions Read the text as students look at the diagram. Have them interact with the text by matching the pictures and the words. Say: Write each word on the lines by the matching picture.

Identify Words

 SEE and SAY (Circle), clap, and count

92

Directions Have students name the images in the picture and circle the picture words that begin with the sound /h/. Then say: Now I will say a sentence about the picture. Listen as I clap for each word: *The hat came off.* There are four words in this sentence. Say other sentences about the picture, and have students identify and count the individual words in each one.

Consonant Hh

MY TURN (Circle)

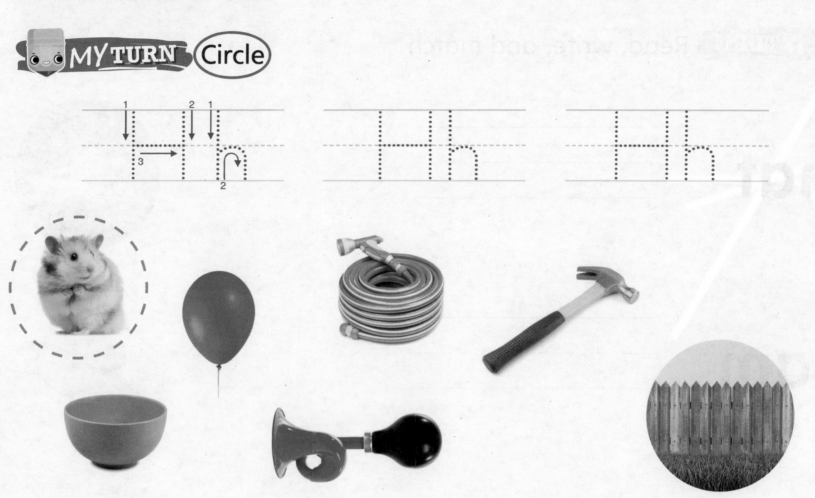

Directions Tell students that the letter *h* makes the sound /h/. Explain that they will see the letter *h* in many words that have the /h/ sound. Model how to form the letters *H* and *h*. Ask students to name the letters at the top of the page and say the sound *h* makes. Then have them trace the letters. Say: Now look at each picture and say its name. Circle the picture words that start with the sound for the letter *h*.

93

Consonant Hh

 **MY TURN** Read, write, and match

hat

_____

- - - - - - - - - - - - - - - - -

_____

ham

_____

- - - - - - - - - - - - - - - - -

_____

hop

_____

- - - - - - - - - - - - - - - - -

_____

Directions Remind students that the letter *h* makes the sound /h/. Ask students to read each word. Then have them write the words on the lines. Finally, have students draw a line from each word to the matching picture.

Sounds

 Circle

Directions Model segmenting a word into individual phonemes: Listen to the sounds in this word: /l/ /o/ /k/. Now, let's blend the sounds to form a word: /l/ /o/ /k/, *lock.* The word *lock* begins with the sound /l/. **Have students segment and blend each picture word in the first row, circling the words that begin with /l/. Continue with the second row and final /l/.**

95

Consonant Ll

 Circle

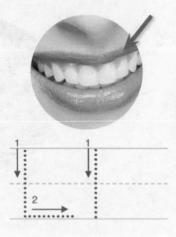

96

Directions Tell students that the letter *l* makes the sound /l/. Model how to form the letters *L* and *l*. Explain that they will see the letter *l* in words that have the /l/ sound. Then have students name each picture. Say: If the picture word begins or ends with the sound for the letter *l*, circle the picture and write the letters.

My Words to Know

one	two	three

My Sentences to Read

 **MY TURN**

I have <u>one</u>.

I have two

Can we have three?

Directions Tell students that the words in the word bank are words they need to practice and remember. Read the high-frequency words with students as they point to each word. Then have students read the sentences and underline the high-frequency words.

Consonant Ll

 Read and write

ap

id

pa

Directions Have students trace the letter *l* in each word. Then have them read the words. Finally, have students write the words on the lines.

The Ham

Highlight the words with the **h** sound.

The ham is hot!

 AUDIO

Audio with Highlighting

ANNOTATE

Hal can have one.

Lin can have two.

Underline the words
with the **I** sound.

Can I have three?

I like ham a lot!

Consonants Hh and Ll

 Read and write

lot	lad	lip
hot	hip	hat
ham	hit	hop
lab	lid	pal

Directions Remind students that the letter *h* makes the sound /h/ and the letter *l* makes the sound /l/. Say: Read the words in the first row. What letter is the same in all three words? Write the letter on the lines. Have students continue with the remaining rows.

Consonants Hh and Ll

 **MY TURN** (Circle) and <u>underline</u>

Lin can (hop).

The lid is hot.

Hal is on my lap.

Look at me hit!

Directions Remind students that the letter *h* makes the sound /h/ and the letter *l* makes the sound /l/. Have students read the sentences. Then have them circle the words that begin with the letter *h* and underline the words that begin with the letter *l*.

103

Read Together

My Learning Goal

I can read about what living things need.

Fiction

Fiction is a make-believe story.

Setting — It is dinnertime.

Characters — The family is at the table.

Plot — They eat ham. They drink water. They feel full!

 TURN and TALK Tell how this story is different from an informational text about what people need.

Directions Read aloud the genre information and model text. Have students identify and describe the characters, setting, and plot, including the main events. Then have them talk about how the story is different from an informational text.

Fiction Anchor Chart

Characters

Setting

Event

Event

Event

Do We Need This?

Preview Vocabulary

food

water

shelter

Read

Read the story to find out what the characters need.

Meet the Author

Guadalupe V. Lopez likes to write about children and their adventures. She gets ideas by watching her own children. When she isn't home writing books, she is in the classroom having fun with her students.

106

Do We Need This?

written by Guadalupe V. Lopez

illustrated by Kathi Ember

 AUDIO

Audio with Highlighting

 ANNOTATE

"Let's go for a hike!" said Mia.
Alex got a map.

CLOSE READ

What is Alex like?
Underline the words
that help you
understand
what he is like.

"This will show us where to go,"
said Alex.
"Now, what do we need?"

"We need this," said Mia.

"No," said Alex. "We need food."

CLOSE READ

What words help you understand what Alex is like? <u>Underline</u> the words.

"We need this," said Mia.
"No," said Alex. "We need water."

"We need these," said Mia.

"No," said Alex. "We don't need all that!"

"Run!" said Alex.
"We need shelter!"

CLOSE READ

How are you like Mia and Alex? Highlight words in the text.

"You are right, Alex," said Mia.
"This is all we really need!"

115

Develop Vocabulary

 **MY TURN** Write

food	water	shelter

Alex and Mia need _____ to eat.

They need _____ to drink.

Directions Read aloud the vocabulary words. Then read the sentences. Have students complete each sentence by writing the correct vocabulary word on the lines. Tell them to use context clues to clarify meanings.

Check for Understanding

 Write

1. What lesson does Mia learn?

_____

- -

_____

2. Why do you think the author wrote this text?

_____

- -

_____

3. Why do people need shelter?

_____

- -

_____

Directions Read aloud the questions one at a time and have students write their responses. Discuss the answers with students.

Identify and Describe Characters

Characters are the people or animals in a story.

 Draw

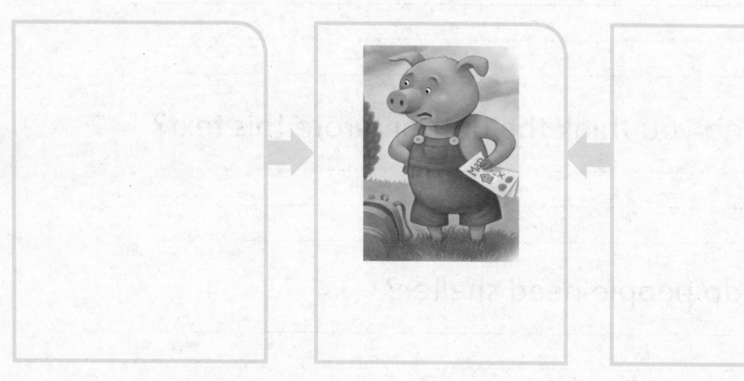

Directions Say: We can describe, or tell about, the main characters in a story. Have students identify the character in the picture. Then have them describe the character by drawing two details about him. Remind students to look back at the text.

Make Connections

 Draw

---

Directions Say: You can connect texts you read to your own life. How are the characters in the story like you? Have students make connections to personal experiences by drawing one way they are like Mia or Alex. Remind students to look back at the text.

Reflect and Share

TURN and TALK What do Alex and Mia need? Retell the story to a partner. Then talk about what a bee needs. How is it similar to what Alex and Mia need?

Weekly Question

How do we know what we need?

120

Directions Have students retell the main events in the story to a partner. Then remind students they read about bees in *From Nectar to Honey*. Say: Bees have needs too. How are a bee's needs like Alex's and Mia's needs? Talk to your partner.

I can use words to make connections.

My Learning Goal

Academic Vocabulary

need	grow	share	depend

 Write

_____

Animals _____ food and water.

_____

Food helps living things _____ big.

Directions Read the sentences one at a time to students. Have them choose the Academic Vocabulary word that best completes each sentence and write it on the lines. Tell students to use clues in the sentences to help them clarify meanings.

Rhyming Sort

 MY TURN Name and draw

Directions Remind students that rhyming words have the same middle and ending sounds. Ask students to name the pictures: *mat, fan, hop.* Then say: I am going to say some words. Draw a picture of each word under the rhyming picture. Say the following words one at a time: *can, hat, top.*

Read Like a Writer, Write for a Reader

 Write

1. Is the person who tells the story a character in the story? Write a clue from the text.

_____

- -

_____

2. Write a sentence about Alex and Mia.

_____

- -

_____

Directions Say: Sometimes the narrator, or the person telling a story, is not a character. The narrator uses the characters' names instead of the word I. Reread a page in the story so students can listen to and experience third-person text. Then read the items one at a time and have students write their responses.

Verbs

A **verb** is an action word.

Some verbs tell about an action that happens now.

The cat **eats**.

The cats **eat**.

 Write

Sam looked at a map.

_____

- -

_____

Directions Say: When a sentence tells about one person or thing, the verb ends with -s. When a sentence tells about more than one person or thing, the verb does not end with -s. Read aloud the sentence at the bottom of the page. Ask students to edit by rewriting the verb on the lines, changing the ending to tell about an action that is happening now.

I can write an informational text.

My Learning Goal

Graphics

A **graphic** shows more information about a main idea.

One kind of graphic is a drawing.

 Draw

Birds need food to eat.

Directions Read aloud the sentence at the top of the drawing box. Say: You can draw a picture to show more information about what birds eat. Have students revise the draft by adding details in a picture.

Words and Sentences

Authors use **words** and **sentences** to tell information.

Letters make up a word.

Words and spaces make up a sentence.

 Circle and underline

home   r   s   food

 Circle

Animals need food and shelter.

Directions Ask students to recognize the difference between a letter and a printed word by circling the letter and underlining the word in each pair. Then ask students to recognize that sentences are comprised of words separated by spaces and recognize word boundaries by circling the spaces between the words in the sentence.

Organize Ideas

Authors **organize** their ideas, or put them in order.

Main Idea → Lots of bugs can fly.

Details → Bees can fly.

Ladybugs can fly too.

🐛 **MY TURN** Organize the ideas in your own writing.

Directions Read aloud the information and model text to students. Have them discuss how the author developed the draft by organizing the ideas. Say: Now you can organize your own writing. Remember to dictate or write your main idea and then list the details.

How Anteaters Eat

An anteater is a kind of animal.

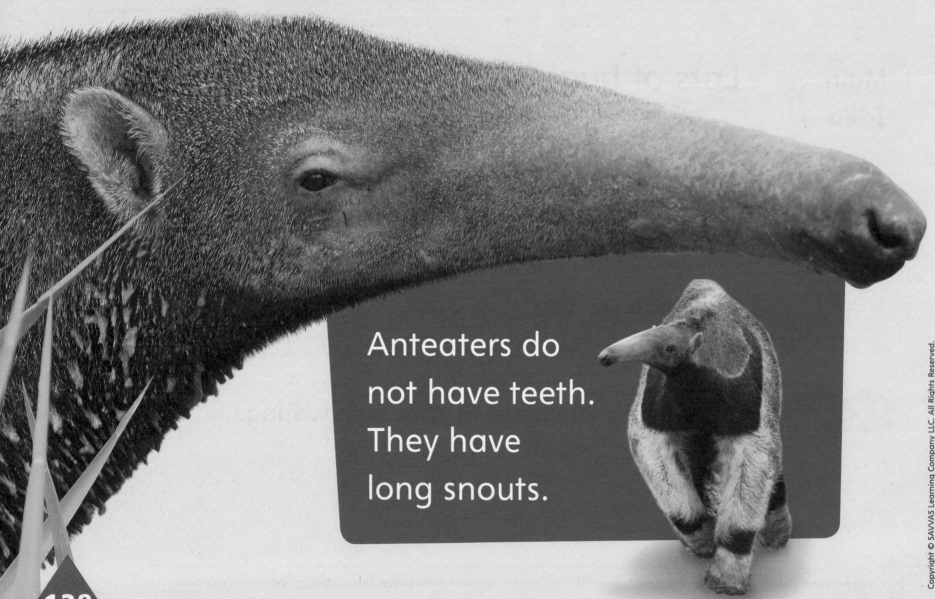

Anteaters do not have teeth. They have long snouts.

Weekly Question

How do different animals eat their food?

Anteaters eat mostly ants and termites. Their long tongues help them eat. They can pick up lots of bugs at once!

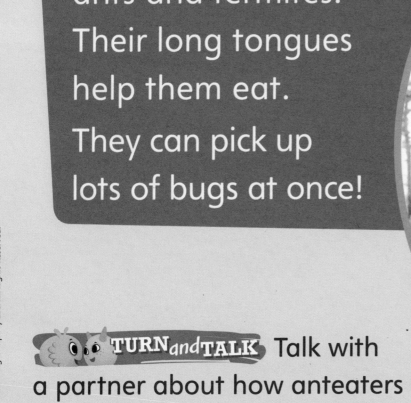

TURN and TALK Talk with a partner about how anteaters eat.

Directions Read aloud the text as students look at the pictures. Have partners discuss what they learned about anteaters.

Sound Parts

 Match

130

Directions Model: Listen to this word: /g/-ate, gate. The word gate begins with the sound /g/. Then have students draw a line to match the picture words in each set that begin with the same sound. Have students segment and blend the onset and rime in each picture word and identify the beginning sound.

Consonant Gg

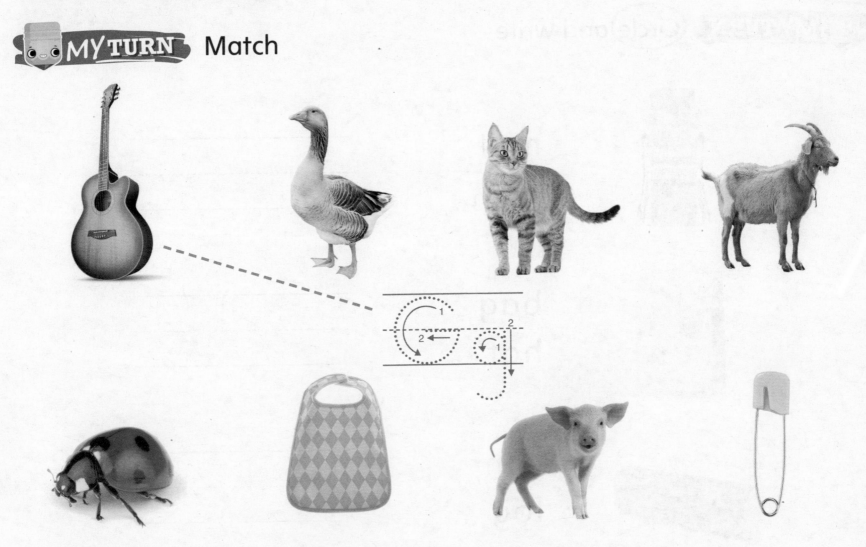 **MY TURN** Match

Directions Tell students that the letter *g* can make the sound /g/. Say: The sound /g/ can be at the beginning or end of a word. You will see the letter *g* in many words that have the /g/ sound. **Model how to form the letters G and g.** Have students trace the letters *Gg* and then draw lines from the letters to the picture words that begin or end with the sound for the letter *g*.

131

Consonant Gg

 MY TURN (Circle) and write

mat
(gas)

bag
hat

can
log

Directions For each item, have students name the picture and tell whether they hear /g/ at the beginning or end. Ask them to circle the word that has the letter for the sound /g/. Then have them read each circled word and write it on the lines.

Blended Sounds

 SEE and SAY Circle

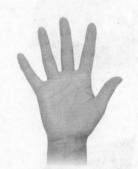

STOP

Directions Model: Listen as I say the sounds in this word: /st/ /e/ /m/. The word begins with the blended sound /st/. Have students identify the sounds in the picture words in the first row and circle the ones that begin with /st/ like *stem*. Continue with the second row and the final blend /nd/.

Consonant Blends

 Match

Directions Say: A consonant blend is two or more consonants that come together at the beginning or end of a word. Their sounds blend together, but each sound is heard. Have students trace the letters and identify the sound each blend makes. Then ask them to draw a line from each pair of letters to the picture word that begins or ends with the same blended sound.

My Words to Know

four	five	here

My Sentences to Read

Here is Pig.

Pig had four.

Pig can see five.

Directions Say: We have to remember and practice some words, such as *here*. Have students read the high-frequency words and then the sentences. Ask them to underline the high-frequency words in the sentences.

Consonant Blends

 Read

mi|k

drop

la|mp

frog

hand

c|ap

Directions Have students name the pictures and trace the letters in each word. Then have them use letter-sound relationships to decode the CCVC and CVCC words. Model the first word: The sound for *m* is /m/. One sound for *i* is /i/. The blended sound for *lk* is /lk/. I will say the sounds together to read the word: /m/ /i/ /lk/, *milk*.

Pig and Frog

Highlight the words with the letter **g**.

Here is Pig at the bin.

He got four.

AUDIO

Audio with Highlighting

ANNOTATE

137

Here is Frog at the pond.

She got five.

138

Underline the words that begin or end with a blend.

Pig and Frog grin.

They are glad!

Consonant Gg and Blends

 **MY TURN** Read and write

got

_____

- - - - - - - - - - - - - - - -

_____

drop

_____

- - - - - - - - - - - - - - - -

_____

spin

_____

- - - - - - - - - - - - - - - -

_____

fast

_____

- - - - - - - - - - - - - - - -

_____

lift

_____

- - - - - - - - - - - - - - - -

_____

pig

_____

- - - - - - - - - - - - - - - -

_____

Directions Have students decode the CVC, CCVC, and CVCC words using letter-sound relationships.
Say: Point to each letter or blend in the word and say the sound it makes. Then say the sounds together
to read the word. **Then have students write the words on the lines.**

Consonant Gg and Blends

 Read

 Gil is with Mom and Dad.

 Look at Gil skip.

 He can skip fast!

 Mom and Dad clap.

Directions Remind students that the letter *g* can make the sound /g/ and a consonant blend is two or more consonants that come together in a word, but each sound is heard. Have students take turns reading the sentences with a partner.

Read Together

My Learning Goal

I can read informational text.

SPOTLIGHT ON GENRE

Informational Text

An informational text has a **title** and **graphics**.

The title tells what the text will be about.

Graphics give more information.

 TURN and TALK Tell a partner what you know about informational texts.

Directions Read the genre information to students and talk about titles and simple graphics, such as photos, illustrations, and maps. Say: Details in the graphics tell more about the central, or main, idea of the text. Have students work with a partner to discuss what they have learned about informational texts.

142

Informational Text Anchor Chart

Text Features

Title

Photo

Farm Animals

Open Wide!

Preview Vocabulary

shark

eagle

turtle

hummingbird

Read

What do you think you will read about in this text?

Meet the Author

Ana Galán was born in Spain. Before she was a writer, Ana worked as a veterinarian. Her favorite animals are dogs and horses. She lives in New York with her family and her dog.

144

Directions Say: You can use the words and picture on the title page to make a prediction, or tell what you think you will read. You can also use the repeating structure of the text to predict what the text will be about. **Have** students make a prediction using text features and structures.

Open Wide!

written by
Ana Galán

 AUDIO

Audio with Highlighting

 ANNOTATE

Animals need food.
What do they eat?

CLOSE READ

What do you think you will read about in this text? Highlight the words that tell you. Use the pictures too.

This bear has a big mouth.
What does it eat?
It eats plants and meat.

This shark has many teeth.
What does it eat?
It eats fish.

CLOSE READ

What body parts do these animals use to eat? Underline the words that tell what the pictures show.

This eagle has a yellow beak.
What does it eat?
It eats meat and fish.

This hummingbird has a long beak.
What does it drink?
It drinks sweet nectar.

How do these animals use their mouths? <u>Underline</u> the words that tell what the pictures show.

This frog has a long tongue.
What does it catch?
It catches tasty insects.

This turtle has no teeth.
What does it nibble?
It nibbles plants.

CLOSE READ

Think about what you predicted the text would be about. Was your prediction correct? Highlight the words that tell what the text is about.

There are all kinds of animal mouths. Different kinds of animals eat different kinds of things!

Develop Vocabulary

 Circle

shark | eagle | turtle | hummingbird

154

Directions Read the vocabulary words to students. Point out that each word is in a different color box. Have students use colors to match the pictures and the words. Say: The word *shark* is in a red box. Draw a red circle around the picture that shows a shark. Have students continue with the remaining words and pictures.

Read Together

Check for Understanding

MY TURN (Circle) and write

1. What kind of graphic does the author use?

| maps | photos |

2. Why does the author tell about different kinds of animals?

_____

- -

_____

3. How are the shark and the turtle different?

_____

- -

_____

Directions Read aloud question 1 and the answer choices to students. Have them circle the answer. Then read aloud questions 2 and 3 and have students write their responses. Remind them to use text evidence.

Find Text Features

 MY TURN Write and draw

_____

- -

_____

Directions Tell students that informational texts have a title that names the topic and simple graphics that give more information. Have students look back at the text. Ask them to write the title and draw two details they learned from the photos. Say: Authors write informational texts to share information. The title and pictures can help them. Discuss how the title and graphics help the author achieve her purpose.

Make and Confirm Predictions

 **MY TURN** Draw and circle

Were you correct?   Yes   No

Directions Remind students that they looked at the title page's words and picture as well as the text's repeating structure to make a prediction about the text. Have them draw what they predicted. Then say: Now that you have finished reading, use what you know to tell if your prediction was correct. Have students confirm their prediction by circling *Yes* or *No*.

Reflect and Share

 TURN and TALK Which animal was the most interesting to learn about? How does that animal eat? What does that animal make you think about?

> It reminds me of _____.

Weekly Question

How do different animals eat their food?

Directions Explain that students can respond to sources by sharing their opinions and describing how ideas in the texts from this week connect to their own lives. Tell students to recall what they learned in *Open Wide!* and *How Anteaters Eat*. Then have them share their opinions and personal connections to the texts with a partner.

Read Together

I can use words to tell about informational text.

My Learning Goal

Academic Vocabulary

grow	need	share	depend

**MY TURN** Write

un	pre	re

The leaves grow again every year.

They _____grow_____.

Directions Say: The word part *un-* means "not." The word part *pre-* means "before." The word part *re-* means "again." Read the sentences to students. Have them think about the meaning of the first sentence. Then have them write the word part that best completes the word *grow* in the second sentence.

Rhyming Sort

 Match

160

Directions Remind students that rhyming words have the same middle and ending sounds. Say: Listen to these words: *hot, clock, lap, rock, cap, knot*. Have students draw a line from each picture word at the top of the page to the picture word at the bottom that rhymes. Then ask them to produce rhyming words by saying other words that rhyme with one of the pairs.

Read Like a Writer, Write for a Reader

 Write

1. What word in the text helps you picture a hummingbird's beak?

_____

Hummingbirds have a _____ beak.

2. What other word can you use to tell about a hummingbird's beak?

_____

Hummingbirds have a _____ beak.

Directions Say: Authors use words that help readers visualize, or picture in their minds, what is happening. Have students discuss words from the text that helped them visualize how animals eat. Read question 1 and have students go back to the text to find the answer. Read question 2 and have students write their response. Encourage them to look back at the photo in the text for ideas.

Verbs

A verb that ends with **ed** tells about an action in the past.

Yesterday I walk**ed**.

 MY TURN (Circle) and write

I talk to Grandma yesterday.

Last fall I start school.

Directions Say: Remember that a verb is an action word. Read aloud the information at the top of the page. Then read the sentences one at a time. Have students edit each sentence by circling the verb and then writing the past-tense form of the verb on the lines.

I can write an informational text.

My Learning Goal

Edit for Singular and Plural Nouns

A **singular noun** names one person, animal, place, or thing.

A **plural noun** names more than one.

 Write

The _____ is green. (frog)

It has two _____. (eye)

It uses its _____ to hop. (leg)

Directions Have students edit each sentence by deciding if the noun in parentheses should be singular or plural. Have them write the correct form of the word on the lines. Then ask students to edit for singular and plural nouns in their list books.

Edit for Capitalization

A complete sentence begins with
a **capital** letter.

 **MY TURN** (Circle) and write

_____

- - - - - - - - - - - - - - - - - - - -

we learned about animals. _____

_____

- - - - - - - - - - - - - - - - - - - -

they have different mouths. _____

_____

- - - - - - - - - - - - - - - - - - - -

all animals need to eat. _____

164

Directions Say: The first letter in a sentence should be a capital, or uppercase, letter. Have students edit by circling the letter in each sentence that should be capitalized. Ask them to write the capital letter on the lines. Then have students edit for capitalization in their list books.

Edit for Adjectives

An **adjective** describes something.

Adjectives can tell about size, color, or shape.

 Write

a _____ shirt

a _____ ball

Directions Have students edit the phrases by thinking of a color, size, or shape word they could add. Have students write the adjectives on the lines. Then ask students to edit their drafts to include adjectives.

165

Let's Exercise!

Exercise is fun!

You can run like a dog.

Exercise is fun!

You can leap like a frog.

Exercise is good for you!

You can be strong like a bear.

Exercise is good for you!

You can be fast as a hare.

166

Why is exercise important?

 **MY TURN** Draw

Directions Read the poem as students look at the pictures. Say: Now you will interact with the poem by drawing a picture about it. Interacting in meaningful ways means you are interacting in ways that help you understand the text. Have students illustrate their favorite way of exercising from the poem.

Middle Sounds

 (Circle)

Directions Model the first word: Listen to the sounds in *web*: /w/ /e/ /b/. *Web* has /e/ in the middle. Have students name each picture and circle the picture words that have the sound /e/ in the middle.

Short e Spelled e

 MY TURN (Circle)

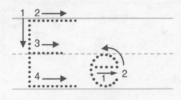  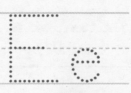 

Directions Tell students that the letter *e* can make the sound /e/. Explain that they will see the letter *e* in many words that have the /e/ sound. Model how to form the letters *E* and *e*. Have students trace the letters *Ee*. Say: Point to the letter *e* and tell me the sound it makes. Then have students name the pictures and circle the ones that have the sound for *e* in the middle.

169

Short e Spelled e

 **MY TURN** Read, write, and draw

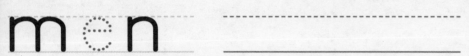

m e n

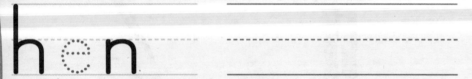

h e n

p e t

Directions Have students trace the letter e in each word. Then have them read each word and write it on the lines. Finally, have students choose one word and draw a picture that shows the word.

Initial Sounds

Directions Say: Listen to the sound at the beginning of this word: /w/ -atch. *Watch* begins with the sound /w/. Now circle and say the picture words in the first row that begin with the same sound as *watch*. Continue with the second row, having students circle and say the picture words that begin with the sound /y/ like *yawn*.

171

Consonants Ww and Yy

 Match

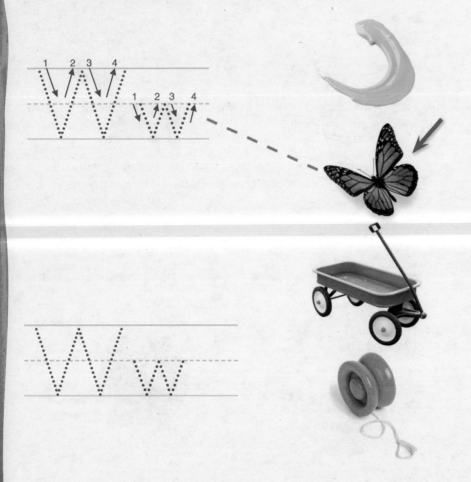

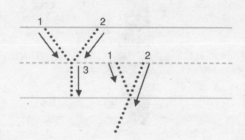

172

Directions Say: The letter *w* makes the sound /w/. You will see the letter *w* in many words that have the /w/ sound. Model how to form the letters *W* and *w*. Have students trace the letters *Ww* and say the sound for the letters. Repeat with the sound /y/ and the letters *Yy*. Then have students draw a line from each set of letters to a picture word that begins with the sound for those letters.

My Words to Know

go	from	yellow

My Sentences to Read

The sled is <u>yellow</u>.

He got it from me.

Look at him go!

Directions Say: There are some words that we have to remember and practice. Listen as I read these words: *go*, *from*, *yellow*. Have students read the high-frequency words. Then have them read the sentences and underline the high-frequency words in the sentences.

173

Consonants Ww and Yy

 MY TURN Read, write, and match

y am

y ak

w ag

w in

174

Directions Remind students that the letter y can make the sound /y/ and the letter w makes the sound /w/. Have students trace the letter y or w in each word and say the sound for the letter. Then have them read the words and write them on the lines. Finally, have students draw a line from each word to the matching picture.

They Can Do It!

Highlight the words that begin with the **w** sound.

Pam can swim with Wil.

They are wet!

AUDIO

Audio with Highlighting

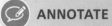
ANNOTATE

175

Wes can go on a yellow sled.

He will not go yet!

Underline the words with the short **e** sound. Highlight the words with the letter **y**.

Sal can bat.

Yes! Look at it go!

177

Short e and Consonants Ww and Yy

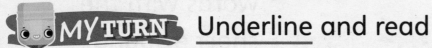 **MY TURN** <u>Underline</u> and read

<u>yes</u>	drop	yet	yam

wet	win	tin	went

10

list	step	let	nest

Directions Have students identify the sound at the beginning of *yo-yo*. Then have them underline the words in the first row that begin with the letter for that sound. Continue with the beginning sound in *wagon* and the middle sound in *ten*. Finally, have students use what they know about letters and sounds to read the CVC, CCVC, and CVCC words.

Short e and Consonants Ww and Yy

 **TURN and TALK** Read

 **I do not have a pet yet.**

The dog is wet!

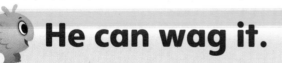 **He can wag it.**

Yes! I will get the dog.

Directions Remind students that the letter *e* can make the sound /e/, the letter *w* makes the sound /w/, and the letter *y* can make the sound /y/. Then have students take turns reading the sentences with a partner.

My Learning Goal

I can read about what living things need.

Persuasive Text

The author of a **persuasive text** wants you to think or do something. A persuasive text has an **opinion** and **reasons**.

Opinion — You should join a soccer team.

Reasons — You will get a lot of exercise.

You will make new friends!

TURN and **TALK** Why did the author write this text? How is it different from an informational text?

Directions Read aloud the genre information. Say: An *opinion* tells what the author wants you to think or do. *Reasons* tell why you should think or do that thing. **Read the model text.** Have students recognize characteristics of the persuasive text and state what the author wants to persuade readers to think or do. Then ask them to discuss how the model text is different from an informational text.

180

Persuasive Text Anchor Chart

Opinion

Reason

Reason

Run, Jump, and Swim

Preview Vocabulary

swim

push

climb

carry

Read

Read the text and look at the pictures to learn about why you should exercise.

Meet the Author

Kimberly Feltes Taylor has written more than 15 books. She likes reading, watching movies, going on long walks, and playing tennis.

182

Run, Jump, and Swim

 AUDIO

Audio with Highlighting

 ANNOTATE

written by Kimberly Feltes Taylor

Why should you exercise?

CLOSE READ

What does the author want us to do? <u>Underline</u> the word.

Exercise is fun.
It gives you strength to carry things.

185

Exercise is fun.
It gives you power to push things.

CLOSE READ

Why does the author think we should exercise? Underline the reasons.

Exercise is fun.
It helps your bones and heart stay strong.

What can you do to exercise?
You can run.
You can climb.

CLOSE READ

What details does the author tell about exercise on these pages? Highlight the important details.

You can jump.
You can swim.

Exercise is fun.
It makes you feel good too.

It is fun to exercise with your friends!

Develop Vocabulary

 MY TURN Circle

(push)   carry   swim   climb

push   climb   carry   swim

Directions Read the words below each picture to students. Have them identify the action shown in the picture and circle the vocabulary word that names the action.

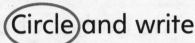 Read Together

Check for Understanding

 **MY TURN** (Circle) and write

1. One opinion the author gives is

_____

- -

_____ .

2. The author would want us to

watch a movie	play baseball

3. What exercises can you do to be strong?

_____

- -

_____

Directions Read aloud the items one at a time and have students circle or write their responses. Remind students to use text evidence.

Find Text Structure

Text structure is how a text is organized. The author of a persuasive text writes an opinion and then gives reasons to convince you to think or do something.

 **MY TURN**   Write and draw

_____

- -

_____

Directions Have students find and read the opinion and reasons in the text. Discuss how this text structure contributes to the author's purpose. Then have students write what the author is trying to persuade the reader to think or do and draw one reason she gives in the text.

Find Important Details

 Draw

Directions Remind students that details tell more about a topic. Say: Finding the most important details will help you better understand what you are reading. Have students evaluate details they learned in the text and draw two important details about exercise. Remind them to look back at the text.

 195

Reflect and Share

 Draw

Weekly Question

Why is exercise important?

196

Directions Tell students they read about exercise. Remind students they have also read about other things people can do to stay healthy. Say: You can respond to a text by drawing a picture that shows how it connects to your own life. Have students describe personal connections by drawing what they can do to stay healthy, including one exercise from the text and something else they have read about.

I can use words to make connections.

My Learning Goal

Academic Vocabulary

grow	need	share	depend

 Write

_____

- -

_____

- -

_____

TURN and TALK Guess the word.

Directions Ask students to write two words they learned in this unit. Then have them draw or act out the words for a partner. Have partners guess each other's words.

Rhyming Sort

 Match

1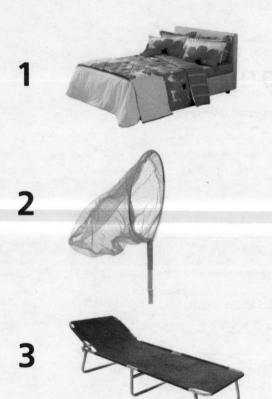

_____

_____

2

- - - - - - - - - - - - - - -

_____

3

- - - - - - - - - - - - - - -

_____

Directions Remind students that rhyming words have the same middle and ending sounds. Have students say each picture word, listening to the middle and ending sounds. Then have them match each picture in the first column with the rhyming picture in the second column by writing the correct number on the line.

Read Like a Writer, Write for a Reader

 Write

1. Find a word in the text that tells why exercise is fun.

_____

- -

_____

2. Write your own sentence that tells why exercise is fun.

_____

- -

_____

Directions Say: An author gives reasons to support a main idea in a text. Read the first item and have students look through the text to find an answer to write on the lines. Have students discuss their responses. Then ask students to write their own reason to support the author's main idea that exercise is fun.

Verbs

A verb that tells about the future has the word **will** before the verb.

I **will push** the cart this afternoon.

 Tell about something you will do later today.

 Cross out

I will climbed the mountain tomorrow.

We will played baseball yesterday.

Directions Read the information and ask students to tell a partner about something they will do later using a future tense verb. Then read aloud the sentences one at a time. Remind students that the ending -ed tells about a past action and the word *will* tells about a future action. Have students decide if each sentence tells about the past or the future and edit the sentence by crossing out -ed or *will*.

200

 **Read Together** **WRITING WORKSHOP**

My Learning Goal

I can write an informational text.

Edit for Prepositions

Authors use prepositions to add details.

A **preposition** is a word that shows a relationship.

 Write

on	in	by

_____

The fish swims _____ the pond.

_____

The tree is _____ the pond.

Directions Say: Some prepositions tell where something is located. Read each sentence and have students edit by writing the best preposition from the word bank on the lines. Ask students to edit their list books for prepositions.

Edit for Capitalization

Authors make sure every sentence begins
with a capital letter.

MY TURN (Circle) and write

_____
- - - - - - - - - - - - - - - - -

we can exercise. _____
_____

- - - - - - - - - - - - - - - - -
It is fun! _____
_____

- - - - - - - - - - - - - - - - -
look at me run. _____
_____

- - - - - - - - - - - - - - - - -
what can you do? _____

202

Directions Have students point to the first word in each sentence and tell if the first letter is capitalized. If it is not, have students edit by circling the letter and writing the capital letter on the lines. Ask students to edit for capitalization in their list books.

Assessment

Here is what you have learned to do in this unit.

- ☐ Write a title

- ☐ Write a central, or main, idea

- ☐ Write details

- ☐ Add details in words

- ☐ Add details in pictures

Directions Read aloud and discuss the list with students. Answer any questions students have about the items. You may wish to review other skills students have learned in this unit as well, such as generating and organizing ideas and editing for capitalization.

UNIT THEME

Living Together

 **TURN and TALK**

Go back to each text and name one thing that living things need. Use the Weekly Questions to help you.

BOOK CLUB

Do We Need This?

How do we know what we need?

Do We Need This?
written by Guadalupe V. Lopez
illustrated by Kathi Ember

WEEK **3**

From Nectar to Honey

WEEK **2**

How do some living things make what they need?

From **Nectar to Honey**
written by Christine Taylor-Butler

BOOK CLUB

Animals on the Move

WEEK **1**

Why do some animals move from place to place?

Animals on the **Move**
written by Ron Fridell

204

Read Together

BOOK CLUB

Open Wide!

How do different animals eat their food?

WEEK 4

BOOK CLUB

WEEK 5

BOOK CLUB

Run, Jump, and Swim

Why is exercise important?

Essential Question

What do living things need?

WEEK 6

Project

Now it is time to apply what you learned about what living things need in your **WEEK 6 PROJECT: Get a Pet!**

Short o Word Families

 Write

hop

_____

_____

dot

_____

_____

206

Directions Have students write the word for each picture. Then have them read each word.

My Words to Know

| blue | what | green |

My Sentences to Read

1. Can you see <u>what</u> I see?

2. I see a green frog.

3. I see a blue pond.

Directions Have students read the high-frequency words. Then have them read the sentences and underline the high-frequency word in each sentence.

Short e Word Families

 Write

men

_____

_____

pet

_____

_____

208

Directions Have students write the word for each picture. Then have them read each word.

What Is Tom?

Highlight the words that are in the same word family as **mom**.

That one is green.

Tom can get it.

 AUDIO

Audio with Highlighting

 ANNOTATE

That big one is blue.

Tom can get it.

Underline the word that is in the same word family as **net**.

What is Tom?

Tom is a bat.

211

Get a Pet!

Talk about the picture. If you could have any pet, what would you get?

 COLLABORATE Our pet is a

_____

- -

_____ .

Directions Have students work together to talk about the pets in the picture and discuss what pet they would like to get.

Use Words

 **COLLABORATE** Work with a partner. Ask each other questions about pets. Use new academic words.

Pet Research Plan

Check each box as you do your project.

☐ Choose a pet.

☐ Research your pet.

☐ Draw and write about your pet.

☐ Share with others.

Directions Help students generate questions about their pet. Say: To ask questions, think of things you need to find out about your pet. One question might be *What does it eat?* Then preview the steps in the research plan. Explain that students will follow the plan by reading and completing each step.

Tell Me About It!

Authors write informational texts to inform, explain, or teach something.

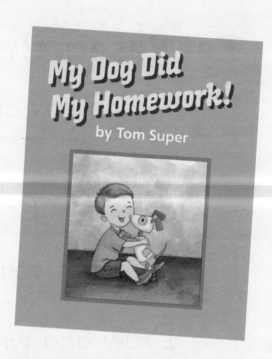

TURN and TALK **Which book is informational? How can you tell?**

Directions Have students review the book covers. Ask partners to talk about which book is an informational text and how they know.

Ask an Expert!

RESEARCH

There are many places to gather information about your pet.

COLLABORATE Circle the sources you will use.

Directions Discuss a variety of sources students can access for research. Tell them to circle the sources they will use. Have students gather information from these sources by taking notes.

Take Notes

What does your pet need?

My bird needs food.

Your pet bird needs food and a home.

 COLLABORATE Write or draw what your pet needs.

Directions Read aloud the research example at the top of the page. Explain that taking notes from a book is one way to gather information. Discuss with students other sources for research. Then have students follow the example to take notes from a variety of sources.

Revise and Edit

Add details to make your writing better.

What kind of food does your pet need?

My bird needs food.

cake   seeds   pasta

My bird needs seeds.

COLLABORATE Write what your pet needs.

_____

My pet needs _____.

Directions Read aloud the information. Have students follow the revision example to make their notes more specific.

Share

Follow the rules for speaking and listening.

Reflect

Did I learn something new?

- -

Did I enjoy this project?

Directions Have students review the rules for speaking and listening before sharing. Ask them to use an appropriate mode of delivery to present their project. After sharing, have students reflect on their project.

Reflect on Your Reading

 Write

I like

Reflect on Your Writing

 Write

My best writing is

Directions Have students share their opinions about what they like and about their best work.

How to Use a Picture Dictionary

This is a picture of the word.

up

This is the word you are learning.

 Draw

Directions Tell students they can use a picture dictionary to find words. The pictures in a picture dictionary show the meanings of the words. Say: The topic of this picture dictionary is **directions and positions**. Look at the pictures as I read the words. Have students identify the word *bottom* and use it in a sentence. Then have them draw a picture that shows the meaning of the word.

Directions and Positions

top

down

front

back

bottom

How to Use Digital Resources

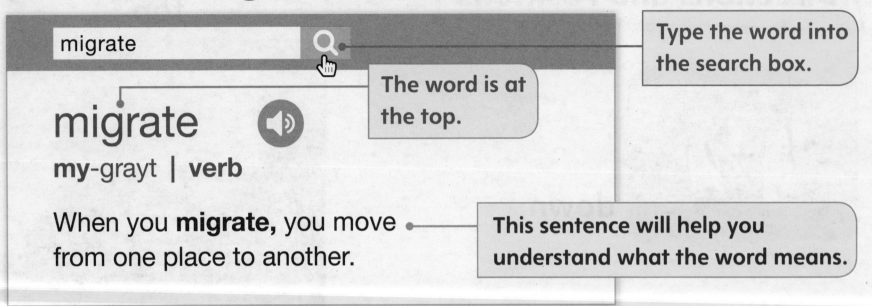

migrate 🔍

Type the word into the search box.

The word is at the top.

migrate 🔊

my-grayt | **verb**

When you **migrate,** you move from one place to another.

This sentence will help you understand what the word means.

 **MY TURN** Draw

222

Directions Say: If a word you are looking for is not in this glossary, you can look for it in an online dictionary or resource. Type the word you are looking for in the search box. When you hit return, the word will appear. Have students find the word *beak* using an online dictionary and draw a picture that shows the meaning of the word.

Bb

bees **Bees** are insects that can make honey.

butterflies **Butterflies** are insects with large, colorful wings.

Cc

carry When you **carry** something, you take it from one place to another.

climb When you **climb**, you use your hands or feet to go up.

Dd

depend When you **depend** on something, you rely on it for support.

223

Ee

eagle An **eagle** is a type of large bird with good vision and powerful wings.

Ff

food **Food** is what living things eat.

Gg

geese **Geese** are a type of bird that swims and has a long neck.

grow When you **grow**, you get bigger.

Hh

hive A **hive** is a nest for bees.

honey Honey is the sticky, sweet liquid that bees make.

hummingbird A **hummingbird** is a small bird with wings that move very fast.

Nn

nectar Nectar is a sweet liquid that is found in many flowers.

need When you **need** something, you cannot do without it.

Pp   **push** When you **push** something, you press against it to make it move.

Ss   **share** When you **share**, you let others use or have something.

shark A **shark** is a large fish with sharp teeth.

shelter A **shelter** is something that covers or protects us.

swim When you **swim**, you use your arms and legs to move through water.

Tt   **turtle** A **turtle** is an animal with a large shell that covers its body.

Ww   **water** **Water** is the liquid living things need to live.

whales **Whales** are large sea animals that breathe through a hole at the top of their head.

CREDITS

Photographs

Photo locators denoted as follows Top (T), Center (C), Bottom (B), Left (L), Right (R), Background (Bkgd)

5 Sharply_Done/Getty Images; 6 DavidTB/Shutterstock; 7 FatCamera/Getty Images; 8 (BL) Sweetcrisis/123RF, (Bkgd) Paolo Costa/Shutterstock; 9 (TL) Sharply_Done/Getty Images, (BCL) DavidTB/Shutterstock, (BL) FatCamera/Getty Images; 10 (CR) Wavebreakmedia/Shutterstock, (BR) Oksana Kuzmina/Shutterstock; 12 (BC) Sufi/Shutterstock, (BL) Richard Peterson/Shutterstock, (BR) 123RF, (C) Shutterstock; 13 Lamseji/Fotolia; 14 (BC) Nancy Bauer/Shutterstock, (Bkgd) Detchana Wangkheeree/Shutterstock, (CR) Connie Barr/Shutterstock; 15 (C) Bergserg/Shutterstock, (BR) Richard Seeley/Shutterstock; 16 (BCL) Room27/Shutterstock, (BCR) Africa Studio/Shutterstock, (BL) Valzan/Shutterstock, (BR) Tehvon/Shutterstock, (TCL) Insago/Shutterstock, (TCR) Hwanchul/Shutterstock, (TL) Lisa A. Svara/Shutterstock, (TR) Ayzek/Shutterstock; 17 (BCL) Diyana Dimitrova/Shutterstock, (BCR) Luis Molinero/Shutterstock, (BL) Deep OV/Shutterstock, (BR) Alex Staroseltsev/Shutterstock, (C) Yunava1/Shutterstock, (CL) Steshkin Yevgeniy/Shutterstock, (CR) Lisa A. Svara/Shutterstock; 18 (BL) Alhovik/Shutterstock, (CL) Luis Molinero/Shutterstock, (TL) Griffin Montgomery/Shutterstock; 19 (BCL) Sergio Schnitzler/Shutterstock, (BCR) Arfa Adam/Shutterstock, (BL) Nick Biebach/123RF, (BR) Fotomaster/Fotolia, (TCL) Africa Studio/Shutterstock, (TCR) Stockagogo, Craig Barhorst/Shutterstock, (TL) Kiri11/Shutterstock, (TR) Volodymyr Krasyuk/Shutterstock; 20 (BC) Roblan/123RF, (BL) Dny3d/Shutterstock, (BR) Panda3800/123RF, (TC) Kaweestudio/Shutterstock, (TL) Anyka/123RF, (TR) Africa Studio/Shutterstock; 22 (B) Michaeljung/Shutterstock, (C) Andrey Popov/Shutterstock, (T) Sataporn Jiwjalaen/123RF; 27 Oksana Kuzmina/123RF; 30 (TL) Richard Ellis/Alamy Stock Photo, (TC) Valentino Visentini/Alamy Stock Photo, (TR) Catmando/Shutterstock; 31 Sharply_Done/Getty Images; 32 SasinTipchai/Shutterstock; 33 (B) Zizar/Shutterstock, (T) Glass and Nature/Shutterstock; 34 Andrew Mayovskyy/Getty Images; 35 Richard Ellis/Alamy Stock Photo; 36 Valentino Visentini/Alamy Stock Photo; 37 Catmando/Shutterstock; 38 (CR) WaterFrame/Alamy Stock Photo, (TCR) Musat/Getty Images, (TR) Skip Moody/Dembinsky Photo Associates/Alamy Stock Photo; 39 Asiseeit/Getty Images; 42 (CL) Andrew Mayovskyy/Getty Images, (C) Asiseeit/Getty Images, (CR) Sharply_Done/Getty Images; 45 John L.

Absher/Shutterstock; 46 (BC) Risteski Goce/Shutterstock, (BL) Kirsanov Valeriy Vladimirovich/Shutterstock, (BR) Eurobanks/Shutterstock, (TC) Deep OV/Shutterstock, (TL) Testing/Shutterstock, (TR) Brooke Becker/Shutterstock; 47 Ethan Daniels/Shutterstock; 48 WaterFrame/Alamy Stock Photo; 52 (C) Mariia Voloshina/123RF, (CR) Irin-k/Shutterstock, (L) StudioSmart/Shutterstock; 53 (L) Steven Ellingson/Alamy Stock Photo, (R) Zhukov Oleg/Shutterstock; 54 (BCL) Domnitsky/Shutterstock, (BCR) Kiri11/Shutterstock, (BL) Dushlik/Shutterstock, (BR) Triff/Shutterstock, (TCL) Deep OV/Shutterstock, (TCR) Africa Studio/Shutterstock, (TL) Africa Studio/Shutterstock, (TR) Philipimage/Shutterstock; 55 (BC) Triff/Shutterstock, (BL) Kiri11/Shutterstock, (C) Domnitsky/Shutterstock, (CL) 123RF, (CR) Fotomaster/Fotolia, (TC) Africa Studio/Shutterstock, (TL) Africa Studio/Shutterstock, (TR) Morenina/Shutterstock; 56 (BL) Domnitsky/Shutterstock, (TL) Africa Studio/Shutterstock; 57 (BCL) Mathisa/Shutterstock, (BCR) Apopium/Fotolia, (BL) Eric Isselee/Shutterstock, (BR) Bogonet/Fotolia, (TCL) Christian42/Fotolia, (TCR) Africa Studio/Shutterstock, (TL) Ruslan Semichev/Shutterstock, (TR) Eric Isselee/Shutterstock; 58 (BC) Sergey Peterman/Shutterstock, (BL) Lukas Godja/Fotolia, (BR) Bogonet/Fotolia, (C) Sondre Lysne/Shutterstock, (CL) Gearstd/Shutterstock, (CR) Apopium/Fotolia, (TC) Irochka/Fotolia, (TL) Christian42/Fotolia, (TR) Sergiy1975/Shutterstock; 60 (BL) Irochka/Fotolia, (CL) Markus Mainka/123RF, (TL) Apopium/Fotolia; 65 (BL) Pro3DArtt/Shutterstock, (BCL) Apopium/Fotolia, (TL) Lisa A. Svara/Shutterstock, (TCL) Africa Studio/Shutterstock; 66 (BC) Olga Khomyakova/123RF, (BL) Yellow Cat/Shutterstock; 68 (TL) MirekKijewski/Getty Images, (TCL) Bildvision AB/Shutterstock, (TCR) Ecosflora/Alamy Stock Photo, (TR) Who What When Where Why Wector/Shutterstock; 69 Wilaiwan Namsuk/Shutterstock; 70 (Bkgd) MirekKijewski/Getty Images, (T) La Gorda/Shutterstock; 71 Zen Rial/Getty Images; 72 (CL) Ecosflora/Alamy Stock Photo, (TR) Arvind Balaraman/Shutterstock; 73 Daniel Prudek/Shutterstock; 74 Who What When Where Why Wector/Shutterstock; 75 StudioSmart/Shutterstock; 76 CL Shaiith/Shutterstock, (TR) Bildvision AB/Shutterstock; 77 PGGutenbergUKLtd/Getty Images; 78 (TR) Bildvision AB/Shutterstock, (TCR) Who What When Where Why Wector/Shutterstock, (BCR) MirekKijewski/Getty Images, (BR) Ecosflora/Alamy Stock Photo; 79 (TC) Shaiith/Shutterstock; 83 (CR) Vetasster/Shutterstock; 84 (BR) Pakhnyushcha/Shutterstock, (CL) Anton Starikov/123RF, (CR) Volodymyr Krasyuk/Shutterstock, (TL) Kiri11/

NOTES